WETLAND FOOD CHAINS

by Rebecca Pettiford

pogo

Ideas for Parents and Teachers

Pogo Books let children practice reading informational text while introducing them to nonfiction features such as headings, labels, sidebars, maps, and diagrams, as well as a table of contents, glossary, and index.

Carefully leveled text with a strong photo match offers early fluent readers the support they need to succeed.

Before Reading

- "Walk" through the book and point out the various nonfiction features. Ask the student what purpose each feature serves.
- Look at the glossary together. Read and discuss the words.

Read the Book

- Have the child read the book independently.
- Invite him or her to list questions that arise from reading.

After Reading

- Discuss the child's questions. Talk about how he or she might find answers to those questions.
- Prompt the child to think more. Ask: What other wetland animals and plants do you know about? What food chains do you think they are a part of?

Pogo Books are published by Jump!
5357 Penn Avenue South
Minneapolis, MN 55419
www.jumplibrary.com

Library of Congress Cataloging-in-Publication Data

Pettiford, Rebecca, author.
 Wetland food chains : who eats what? / by Rebecca Pettiford.
  pages cm. – (Who eats what?)
 Includes index.
 ISBN 978-1-62031-305-3 (hardcover: alk. paper) –
ISBN 978-1-62496-357-5 (ebook)
 1. Wetland ecology–Juvenile literature. 2. Food chains (Ecology)–Juvenile literature. 3. Wetland animals–Juvenile literature. I. Title.
 QH541.5.M3P48 2016
 577.68–dc23

                                        2015030922

Series Editor: Jenny Fretland VanVoorst
Series Designer: Anna Peterson
Photo Researcher: Anna Peterson

Photo Credits: All photos by Shutterstock except:
123RF, 12-13; age fotostock, 14-15; C.C. Lockwood, 20-21b; iStock, 18; Nature Picture Library, 20-21bm; SuperStock, 16-17; Thinkstock, 4, 5, 20-21tm.

Printed in the United States of America at Corporate Graphics in North Mankato, Minnesota.

TABLE OF CONTENTS

CHAPTER 1

STILL WATERS

Welcome to the wetland! The water in this **biome** is still. It can be fresh or salty. It is not deep.

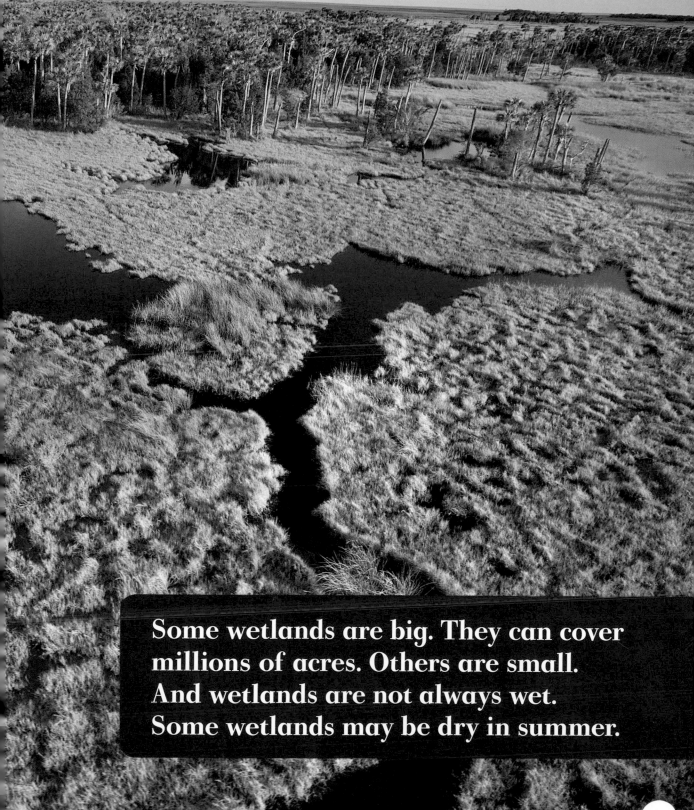

Some wetlands are big. They can cover millions of acres. Others are small. And wetlands are not always wet. Some wetlands may be dry in summer.

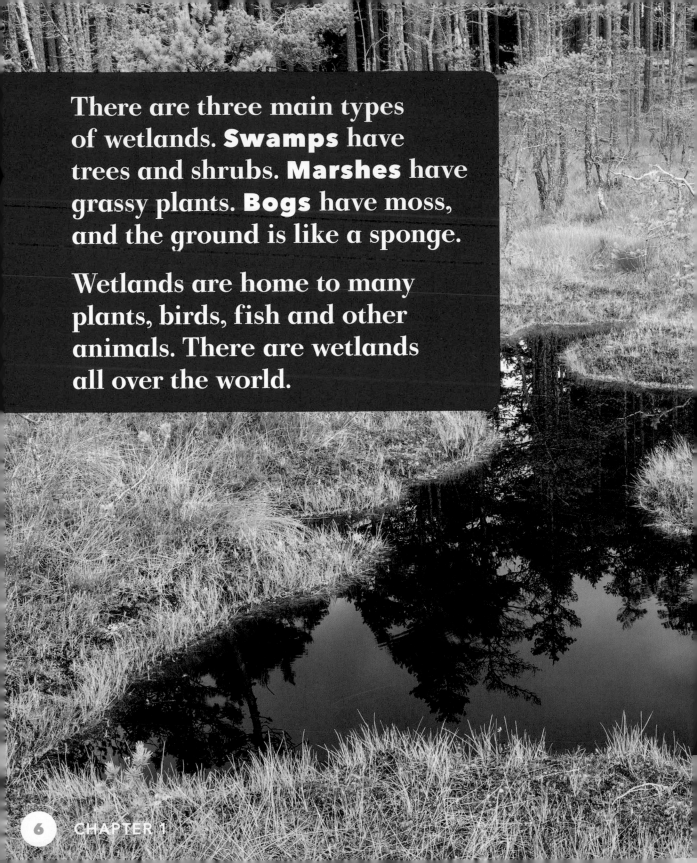

There are three main types of wetlands. **Swamps** have trees and shrubs. **Marshes** have grassy plants. **Bogs** have moss, and the ground is like a sponge.

Wetlands are home to many plants, birds, fish and other animals. There are wetlands all over the world.

WHERE ARE THEY?

Wetlands are found in almost every region of the world. This map shows 10 of the most important wetlands.

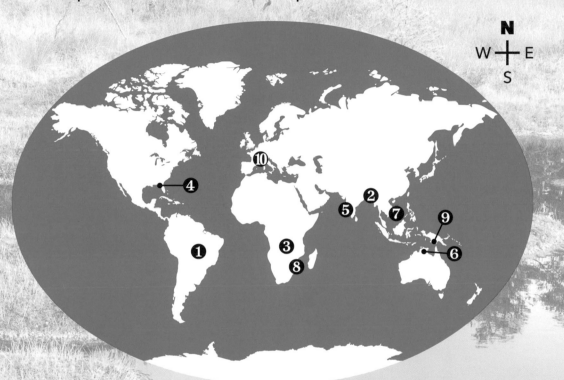

1 = Pantanal

2 = Sundarbans

3 = Okavango Delta

4 = Everglades National Park

5 = Kerala Backwaters

6 = Kakadu National Park

7 = Mekong Delta

8 = iSimangaliso Wetland Park

9 = Wasur National Park

10 = Camargue

CHAPTER 2

THE WETLAND FOOD CHAIN

Like all living things, wetland plants and animals need energy to live. Food is energy. Plants make food from the sun, soil, and water. Animals eat plants and other animals.

A **food chain** shows how energy moves from plants to animals. Each living link in the chain uses or eats the one before it.

cattail
(producer)

Wetland plants like grasses
and cattails are **producers**.
They use energy from the
sun, soil, and water to make
their own food.

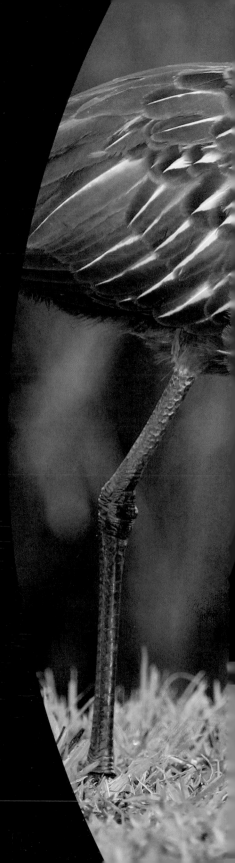

Bacteria and other tiny life forms eat the plants. **Larvae**, snails, and worms eat these life forms. They in turn are eaten by frogs, small fish, and birds.

All of these animals are **consumers**.

limpkin
(predator)

snail
(consumer)

alligator
(top predator)

raccoon
(predator)

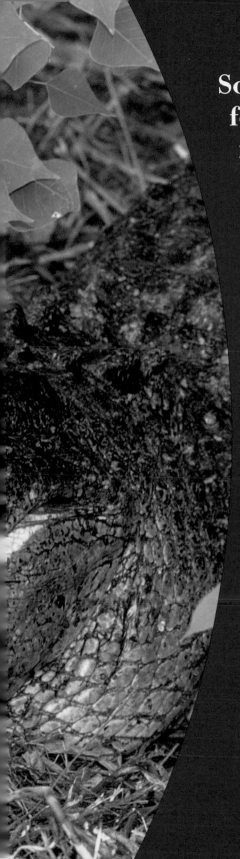

Some consumers become food for **predators** such as raccoons, hawks, and egrets. Large predators will also eat smaller predators. In some wetlands, alligators are at the top of the food chain. They are called top predators. No one messes with them!

DID YOU KNOW?

The Florida Everglades is the largest freshwater marsh in the United States. If you visit, watch out for sawgrass plants. The blades have sharp, jagged edges that can cut your skin!

Decomposers are the last link in the wetland food chain. These organisms break down once-living matter. They return the nutrients to the soil. Vultures, beetles, and flies make up this link. So do mushrooms.

black vulture (decomposer)

One wetland food chain might look something like this:

Producer:
Grass

Predator:
Raccoon

Consumer:
Turtle

Decomposer:
Fly

CHAPTER 3

FOOD CHAIN CLOSE-UPS

Let's look at a food chain. A plant grows in a marsh. An insect larva eats the plant. A dragonfly eats the larva.

A frog eats the dragonfly. A heron eats the frog. In time, the heron dies. Decomposers break down its body. The dead matter returns to the wetland as nutrients.

Let's look at another food chain.

1) Plants grow in a swamp.

2) A crayfish eats the plants.

3) A raccoon eats the crayfish.

4) When the raccoon dies, decomposers break down its body. The nutrients return to the soil.

The food chain continues!

DID YOU KNOW?

Every year, more wetlands disappear. People drain them to build homes and roads. Wetlands are important! Like sponges, they soak up extra water. This helps stop flooding. They keep our drinking water clean. So governments are passing laws to save wetlands.

ACTIVITIES & TOOLS

MAKE A WETLAND

A wetland collects water. It helps stop flooding. Let's see how it works. You will need:

- modeling clay
- an 11 × 7-inch (28 × 18-centimeter) foil pan
- a dry kitchen sponge
- water in a watering can

❶ Use the clay to make a slope in the foil pan. It should cover half the pan. This is your "land." The other half of the pan has nothing in it. This is your "lake."

❷ Slowly pour water (rain) on the clay (land). What happens? Is there a lot of water in your lake?

❸ Empty the water from the pan. Put the sponge in the pan at the land's base. The sponge is the wetland between the land and the lake. Slowly pour water on the land again. What happens? Did the sponge (wetland) soak up some of the water?

GLOSSARY

bacteria: Tiny life forms that break down dead plants and animals.

biome: An area on the earth defined by its weather, land, and the type of plants and animals that live there.

bogs: Areas of wet, spongy ground that have moss.

consumers: Animals that eat plants.

decomposers: Life forms that break down dead matter.

food chain: A way of ordering plants and animals in which each uses or eats the one before it for energy.

larvae: The newly hatched, wingless form of many insects.

marshes: Areas of low, wet land that have grassy plants.

predators: Animals that hunt and eat other animals.

producers: Plants that make their own food from the sun.

swamps: Areas of low, wet land that have trees and shrubs.

INDEX

TO LEARN MORE

Learning more is as easy as 1, 2, 3.

1) **Go to www.factsurfer.com**

2) **Enter "wetlandfoodchains" into the search box.**

3) **Click the "Surf" to see a list of websites.**

With factsurfer, finding more information is just a click away.

gunnison county
Libraries
connect. discover. imagine. learn.

Gunnison Library
307 N. Wisconsin, Gunnison, CO 81230
970.641.3485
www.gunnisoncountylibraries.org